MOMENTS OF GRACE

INSPIRATIONAL GOD-CENTERED HAIKU

CHERYLANNE ARNOTT

Copyright © 2018 by Cherylanne Arnott.

All rights reserved. No part of this publication may be reproduced, distributed, or transmitted in any form or by any means, including photocopying, recording, or other electronic or mechanical methods, without the prior written permission of the author, except in the case of brief quotations embodied in critical reviews and certain other noncommercial uses permitted by copyright law.

Printed in the United States of America

ISBN: Paperback: 978-1-949362-18-3
        eBook: 978-1-949362-17-6

STONEWALL PRESS
PAVING YOUR WAY TO SUCCESS

Stonewall Press
363 Paladium Court
Owings Mills, MD 21117
www.stonewallpress.com
1-888-334-0980

I dedicate this book to my beloved Auntie Marianne.

She instilled in me my passion for the written and spoken word (by teaching me to read and write) as well as for music and motion. Because she has been a constant "grace" in my life for over sixty years, I dedicate this book to her with thanks and love.

ACKNOWLEDGMENT

I wish to recognize and thank my Wonderful Family and my Incredible Friends for their ongoing Support, Critiques, and Enthusiasm in this and all my Endeavors.

I wish to thank my son, Nicolas, my Aunt Marianne and Uncle Vince, my cousin, Dr. Vince, my friend Lallona, my friends Dean and Paula, Sarah; my anchor and advisor, and my illustrator, Juliana.

And I wish to thank Stonewall Press for their Patience, Guidance, Input, and Creativity in bringing my Dream to Life!!!

I can't move Mountains... but I Know
Someone Who Can!! Just leave it to Him!
I Hope my Readers will derive Insight, Inspiration,
and Comfort from 'Moments of Grace' You
are Never Alone: Believing is Seeing!

Readers Comment

'Some get me thinking...Some make me cry...you paint amazing pictures and stir deep emotions with very few words...Keep Writing!!'   ---Nancy

'Some of these make my hair stand on end!'   ---Sarah

'You have a way with words that unlocks and expands the mind...and soul!'   ---Carrie

Author's Comment

I just love and appreciate when God writes Through my hand. I know when He does because it's perfect on the first copy and needs no editing.

Even though I know I'm only the Conduit, (because it's always from Him... just Through me) when that happens: its Rapture... there are no words to describe the Sacred and Harmonious Alliance that's so Evident and Resonating.

I only Reflect His Glory.

Let the warmth of God's Truth Infuse you!

I Speak... He Listens.
...He Answers: I'm Listening.
He Dictates: I Write.

...in my Secret Heart
the Search... has come Full-Circle;
all roads... lead to Him.

Angels... on the Wind...
a World... of Private Music
...Language of the Soul.

this Moment; this Chance;
filled... with Possibilities...
...a New Dawn Rising.

take Life as it comes...
...Heaven IS a Place on Earth;
Garden... of Delight.

Faith... is Ignited:
so Strong: so Simple: so Deep:
...Colors... of the Soul.

He's Calling to me:
with every Beat of my Heart
I Hear... the Magic.

in Moments of Grace
all the Music of Laughter
provides Sweet Relief

He... is like Lightning:
with Sudden Thunder and Fire
...melting into me.

Tempered by the Fire:
...now... All Things are Possible:
Divine Alignment.

Walking in the Light
with Wild Exhilaration:
a State... of Rapture.

sudden Rush... of Hope:
renewed Purity... of Soul...
almost... Jubilant.

God's Always with me.
...loved Him a Thousand Lifetimes:
I'm Never Alone.

Compelled to follow
a Wordless, Silent Summons
into the Temple.

call of the Mountains:
Ascension... to Sacred Space;
Glimpse... of the Divine.

Voices from Heaven
Angelic Circle Chorale...
Lullaby... from Home.

Drifting inside Dreams
Angelic Wings surround me
in the State of Grace.

Come into the Light...
undergo a Tidal Change:
Blossoming Breakthrough.

Angelic Embrace:
Sweet, Dissolving Edge of Bliss:
Grace. Personified.

Early Morning Snow:
Diamonds... falling from the Sky;
Glimmerings of Grace.

having Claimed my Heart,
He's Resurrected my Soul:
the Phoenix Rises.

that Touch of Magic:
the Life Source Invigorates
Despite the Darkness.

bring to Consciousness
{just beyond the Obvious}
what lies Underneath.

my Soul is Alive:
as Radiant as Gemstones...
Beauty to Unveil.

Passion and Brilliance:
Woman is Creation's Crown,
Color, and Detail.

Inner Reflections
finding Grace... in the Silence:
come to Consciousness.

Descent. Death. Rebirth:
Triumph through Adversity.
Rising... from the Smoke.

Move Beyond Fear:
Sacrifice the Illusions:
Trust Divine Timing.

I've been Crowned with Grace,
Refreshment, Laughter, and Rest:
to Heal. and Restore.

Trusting through the Tears
with Courage and Transcendence:
Joy comes at Morning.

I am Not Alone:
as God's Grace Firmly Holds me
Deliverance Comes.

the Soul's Connection:
Strong enough to Withstand Change
in the Line of Fire.

be Glad... and Rejoice:
see things from God's Perspective
Trust Him... to Use You!!

As I fall Asleep
Within my Angel's Embrace
i'll Always be Safe.

Occasions of Joy:
Feathers... on the Breath of God:
Evidence... of Grace.

Deeper Walks with God:
Unconditional Support:
Refreshed Energy.

Eternal Comfort...
the Umbrella of God's Grace
Strong... and Enduring.

Celebrate Moments
Cultivate a Grateful Heart
Enjoy the Journey!

with Childlike Faith
I Observe God's Fingerprints:
Glorious Splendor!

get back Perspective
become as Little Children
Play... and Celebrate!!

walking through the Fire Burns,
yet it's Tempering the Steel
of Final Resolve.

when the Dark Days Come
Hold on… and Ride out the Storm:
you're being made Whole.

Source of Reflection:
the Sacred… is Everywhere.
{what makes your Soul Sigh?}

Transformative Years:
Brutal… but Necessary:
the Wisdom Engraved.

Grace. Delight. Mercy.
Deeper Waters of the Soul
Worthy of Pursuit.

have Courage... be Kind:
the Essence of Existence
in this Fallen World.

Body. Soul. Spirit...
Restoration has Begun:
...the Sacred Romance.

Grateful, and Relieved
I have 'Struck Gold'... in my Friends:
Strength... and Peace of Mind.

to Stand what one Sees
through the Riches of God's Grace:
Profound Magnitude.

the Depth of Friendship:
Faithfulness and Loyalty
through Demanding Times.

Count to three... and Pray.
this Sacred Realm of Silence
Circumvents the Stress.

throw Fear to the Wind;
be Content with what you Have;
God will Follow Through.

a Moment of Grace...
among life's Greatest Delights...
Moonlight on Water.

Everlasting Love...
God's Waiting... to be Wanted.
{there's Room for my Soul}

Intimate Allies:
Powerfully Redemptive
in our Broken World.

through the Vicissitudes
Rivers of Light are Unveiled:
Possibilities...

Access God's Wisdom:
opening up the Passage
to Reveal... and Heal.

the Eternal Light:
He is Love... in it's Essence;
Exploding with Joy!

let God Romance you.
in the Midst of the Madness...
Ask... and Surrender.

mirroring the Soul
only Dreams give Birth to Change
in the Dark of Night.

let Him Carry you:
the Soul's Invincible Strength
a Circle of Grace.

let things take their Course...
this Transcendent Awareness
Repose... of the Soul.

Sparkling Jewels
Angels Dancing on Water
in Wind and Sunlight.

always Eternal
the Essence of God's Goodness
a Whiff... of Eden.

be Grateful to God:
the True Source of Happiness
in the Here and Now.

Believing... is Seeing:
Waiting on a Miracle:
Ask... and then Receive!

the Concept of Flow:
allow Possibilities...
they're all States of Grace.

Seek Divine Guidance
Listening... to the Silence
just begin to Pray.

Always Trust the Lord:
the Sustainer Beside you:
Divine Protection.

Suddenly... there's Light!
God is my greatest Romance:
the Source... of my Joy!!

Enduring Throughout...
Truth... with Strength and Dignity
cannot be Shaken.

the Essence of Soul:
Celebrate Victories in
Everyday Edens.

an Awakening:
every day's worth a Party
...because All... is Grace.

we are Protected:
Celestial Benedictions...
Divine Sustenance.

Ultimate Secret:
True Light's Never Extinguished:
...it's Sacred Soulcraft.

a Rock-Solid Trust:
Faith's the only True Shelter...
it Deepens... and Lasts.

if you only Look
Miracles are Everywhere:
His Light's Shining Through.

through utter Darkness
there is a Light that's Shining:
put your Trust in Him.

through Mazes of Doubt
Trust in Him: Absolutely:
He'll make your Path Straight.

I can't move Mountains
...but I know Someone Who Can!
...just Leave it to Him!!

Realization:
through life's Trials come Blessings:
Speechless... with Surprise!

Jesus is my Strength.
this Ultimate Love Affair
Shelter... from the Storm.

Extreme Paradox:
Broken things become Blessed things:
Divine Alchemy.

in your walks with Him
He's looking for Persistence
along Paths of Trust.

His Power alone
can spin the Straw into Gold:
hold His Hand... and Trust.

His Enduring Love
Slaking the Thirst of my Soul
through the Timelessness.

whisper Jesus' Name;
Pure. Powerful. and Potent:
a quick Thrust of Trust.

Radiant with Love
His Robes of Light Cocoon me
...I am Sanctified...

Honoring One's Soul:
it's where the Healing Begins
...with Deep Gratitude.

You're Always With Me:
my Safe Haven, and Delight,
Overwhelming Love.

give 2nd Chances
display Strength... take Action:
be First... to Forgive.

share Affirmations,
Spiritual Perspectives...
Bathed... in the Oneness.

Tears of Surrender:
Miracles of Forgiveness
flooded with Relief.

learn to Hear His Voice;
look Inside... and Awaken...
finding Peace of Mind.

let His Will be Done.
Trust Him: Watch what He can Do!!
...and All Shall be Well.

just Whisper His Name...
count on Divine Sustenance:
His Armor's the Best!

like the Night Moth's Wings
Laughter Rises to Heaven
Dancing... in the Light.

We're Children of God:
Enjoy Peace in His Presence.
Live... in the Garden.

All's Right with the World...
clinging to His Hand for Strength
we are Delivered.

a Place without Noise:
in the midst of the Maelstrom
the Lord Protects us.

Thankful Attitudes...
Chances... to Grow into Grace
through Uplifting Words.

I have been Gifted;
He is With me, and Within
...Constant Companion.

both Rhyme and Reason
He's the Anchor of my Soul:
a Firm Foundation.

Fierce and Enduring
Trust... in Him... shall be your Strength:
Shelter of the Soul.

be Compassionate.
hold out Golden Chords of Hope;
it sets People Free.

We're Children of Light
attended to by Angels;
Guarded by God's Peace.

Jesus Intercedes
like a Whisper in the Wind.
Help. in Helplessness.

it's my Conviction
there is ever-present Help;
...if you only Ask.

this Loving Promise;
His Luminous Veil of Light
...a Consistent Fire.

the Soul's Voice speaking
lullabies of Thankful Thoughts
through Songs of the Heart.

a Joyful Up-look;
carry His Stillness with you...
a Blanket of Love.

a Passionate Life:
Celebrate All of your Days
with Strength and Action.

Radiate Blessings.
make Someone's Day... make them Smile;
Life-Force Energy.

Trust God in Tough Times
to find your Way through the Night.
then His Grace will Heal.

to Dream and to Grow,
the Harrowing of the Soul is
Something Essential.

Believe. Then Receive
Resurrection of Spirit.
and be Filled... with Joy!!

Lifelong Friendships are
Sacred Dimensions of Soul.
Indispensable.

the Secret Package;
Heaven's hidden in the Heart;
Sealed with His Promise.

Constant. and Perfect.
the Light of His Presence Shines
Brightly in our World.

Time. Help. Courage,
open Windows to Heaven:
Keys... to the Kingdom.

Fragile and Exposed...
Jesus helps us in our Weakness;
Covers us... with Grace.

Touched by a Angel
in Rose-Colored Radiance:
Protection... and Peace.

Relinquish Control.
God's in the Eye of the Storm;
Hope... from Brokenness.

Meditative States
find Entry... to the Secret
through Silent Echoes.

His Voice in your Heart
an Incredible Treasure:
Personal Rapture.

Stronghold of Stillness;
follow God; and Trust His Plan.
...Triumphant Success.

His Truth... is our Light.
in Adversity's Darkness
our Refuge and Strength.

to Walk Alongside
the Living One... Who Sees you...
a Lifelong Affair.

www.ingramcontent.com/pod-product-compliance
Lightning Source LLC
Chambersburg PA
CBHW021200080526
44588CB00008B/430